Volume 2: The Spanish Ships – The Fleets in action – The Battles

From the same author, at Talma Studios:

– *The Mystery of the Ancient Maps - Those extraordinary anomalies which question the history of humanity*
– *Muslims in America in the Time of the Prophet - The evidence on ancient maps?*

– *L'Arme environnementale* (end of 2017) ;
– *Le Mystère des cartes anciennes - Ces anomalies extraordinaires qui remettent en question l'histoire de l'humanité* ;
– *Les Musulmans en Amérique au temps du Prophète - La preuve par les cartes anciennes ?*

– *El misterio de los mapas antiguos - Extraordinarias anomalías que cuestionan la historia de la humanidad*
– *Los musulmanes en América en los tiempos del Profeta - ¿La prueba a través de los mapas antiguos?*

Talma Studios
60, rue Alexandre-Dumas
75011 Paris – France
www.talmastudios.com
info@talmastudios.com

ISBN: 979-10-96132-20-1

Patrick Pasin

SPANISH-AMERICAN WAR
IMAGES OF THE SHIPS

Volume 1: The U.S. Navy

VOL. XLIX. No. 1257.   PUCK BUILDING, New York, April 6th, 1901.   PRICE TEN CENTS.

Copyright, 1901, by Keppler & Schwarzmann.

Puck

Entered at N. Y. P. O. as Second-class Mail Matter.

COLUMBIA'S EASTER BONNET.

TABLE OF CONTENTS

VOLUME 1

THE U.S. NAVY

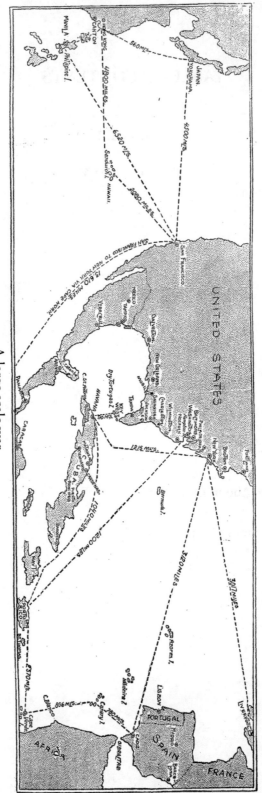

A large scale war

Introduction

About 120 years after the Spanish-American War, we publish this book of images of the ships which made this war. Most pictures come from our extensive collection of documents and newspapers of that time. Some of these images are not very much known, all the more when they stem from Spanish and French sources (*Blanco y Negro*, *L'Illustration*, etc.).

Our goal was not to be exhaustive since many ships took part in this war at various levels, and the material is sometimes no more available or of a quality not good enough to be reproduced, even when we tried miracles to improve it.

Nevertheless, the main ships which were decisive to win this war involving three continents are here. Of course, symbolically, we will start with the *Maine*.

Let's add that the legends under the pictures are the original ones, and it is time now to look at these technological marvels of the 19th century.

USS *Maine*

1) BATTLESHIPS

USS *Maine*
A second-class battleship
Authorized: 1886

Displacement, 6,682 tons.   **Speed,** 17.45 knots.
Complement, 374.
Guns: Main battery, four 10-in., six 6-in.; secondary rapid-fire battery,
seven 6-pounders, eight 1-pounders, four Gatlings.
Torpedo tubes, four.
Destroyed in Havana Harbor, February 15, 1998.

Launching of the *Maine* at
Brooklyn Navy Yard, New York in 1890

The *Maine* in dry dock before her fatal cruise to Havana

Marina de guerra de los Estados Unidos.—EL CRUCERO ACORAZADO «MAINE», DE 6,000 TONELADAS

THE UNITED STATES SHIP MAINE ENTERING HAVANA HARBOR, JANUARY 25, 1898.

From a photograph by John C. Hemment.

10

The *Maine* saluting the Spanish flag after making fast
to the official buoy, at which she was destroyed

In Havana Harbor before the explosion

In Havana Harbor before the explosion

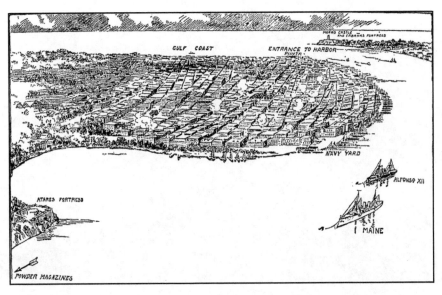

MAINE BLOWN UP!

Terrific Explosion on Board the United States Battleship in Havana Harbor Last Night.

MANY WERE KILLED, DROWNED AND WOUNDED, AND THE BIG WAR SHIP TOTALLY DESTROYED.

City of Havana Shaken to Its Foundations, and Windows Were Broken in All the Houses.

EXPLOSION TOOK PLACE WHEN ALL WERE ASLEEP AND THE SAILORS CAN GIVE NO EXPLANATION AS TO THE CAUSE.

SPANISH CRUISER ALFONSO XII. RENDERED VALUABLE AID WITH HER BOATS—LIGHT HOUSE TENDERS AT KEY WEST ORDERED TO THE SCENE OF THE DISASTER.

A Few Pieces of the Vessel's Equipment Are Still Above Water—All Officers Believed to be Safe and Many Sailors Rescued by Small Boats.

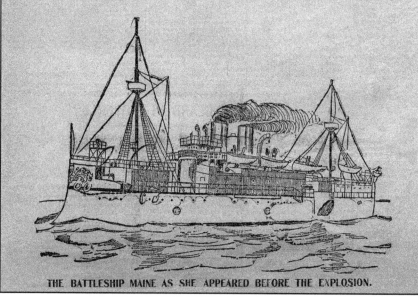

THE BATTLESHIP MAINE AS SHE APPEARED BEFORE THE EXPLOSION.

In *The World*, 17 February 1898

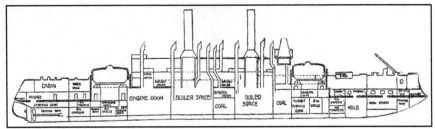

Sectional view–The explosion occurred in the magazine forward

Spanish divers at work outside the wreck of the *Maine*

RESTOS DEL ACORAZADO MAINE EN LA BAHÍA DE LA HABANA
DESPUÉS DE LA EXPLOSIÓN

(De fotografía directa.)

THE NATION'S NAVAL PROGRAM

WILL CEASE TO BE PACIFIC AND BECOME DECIDEDLY AGGRESSIVE

Porto Rico Will Be Left Open for Anchorage if the Spanish Flotilla
Gathers Courage to Cross the Atlantic and Risk an
Engagement With the United States Fleet

USS *Texas*
A second-class battleship
Authorized: 1886

Displacement, 6,315 tons.   **Speed,** 17.8 knots.
Complement, 389.
Guns: Main battery, two 12-in., six 6-in. slow-fire; secondary rapid-fire battery, six 1-pounders, four 37-mm. Hotchkiss, two Gatlings.
Torpedo tubes, two.

3 August 1898

Crewmen in 1898

USS *Indiana*
A first-class battleship
Authorized: 1890

Displacement, 10,288 tons.   **Speed**, 15.5 knots.
Complement, 473.
Guns: Main battery, four 13-in., four 6-in. slow-fire; secondary rapid-fire battery, twenty 6-pounders, six 1-pounders, four Gatlings.
Torpedo tubes, two.

Bow view

In summer 1898

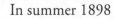

Forward turret, looking aft from the bow

View from top of 8-inch gun turret, looking forward

13-inch guns swung to starboard

The starboard quarters, showing the 13-inch, 8-inch and 6-inch guns

Ramming home the charge in a 13-inch gun

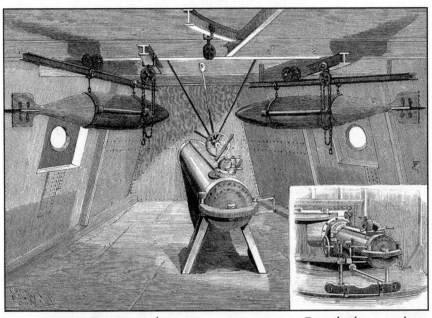

Bow torpedo room

Broadside torpedo tube

Loading the ammunition hoists for 13-inch guns

Breech of the 13-inch guns

Broadside 6-pounder rapid-fire battery

A 100,000 candle power search light

After the fight.
The battle-flags are still flying,
and Spanish prisoners are seen on the deck.

USS *Iowa*

A first-class sea-going battleship
Authorized: 1892

Displacement, 11,340 tons   **Speed**, 17.1 knots
Complement, 505.
Guns: Main battery, four 12-in., eight 8-in., six 4-in. rapid-fire; secondary rapid-fire battery, twenty 6-pounders, four 1-pounders, four Colts, two field guns.
Torpedo tubes, four.

Launching of the *Iowa*

The *Iowa* taking the sea

Crewmen pose (1898)

Running trials

THE AMERICAN BATTLESHIP "IOWA"

THE "IOWA," THE PRIDE OF OUR NAVY, OUTCLASSES THEM ALL.

USS *Massachusetts*
A first-class battleship
Authorized: 1890

Displacement, 10,288 tons.   **Speed**, 16.2 knots.
Complement, 473.
Guns: Main battery, four 13-in., eight 8-in., four 6-inch, slow-fire; secondary battery, twenty 6-pounders, four 1-pounders, four Gatlings, two field guns.
Torpedo tubes, three.

Side view and deck plan of the *Indiana*, *Massachusetts* and *Oregon*
(Aft guns show maximum fire as originally proposed.
Forward guns show maximum fire as finally modified.)

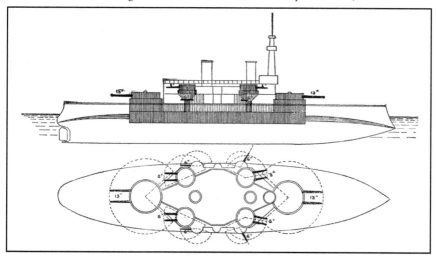

One of the twin engines of the Massachusetts

USS *Oregon*
A first-class battleship
Authorized: 1890

Displacement, 10,288 tons   **Speed**, 16.8 knots.
Complement, 473.
Guns: Main battery, four 13-in., eight 8-in., four slow-fire 6-inch; secondary rapid-fire battery, twenty 6-pounders, six 1-pounders, four Gatlings, two field guns.
Torpedo tubes, three.

(Photographed at full speed)

Leaving for Manila

Returning from Cuba

Crew of the *Oregon*'s starboard forward 8-inch turret, during the chase of the *Colón*, watching the work of the forward 13-inch turret

13-inch gun turret closeup

USS *Kearsarge* and *Kentucky*
First-class battleships
Authorized: 1895

Displacement, 11,525 tons.   **Speed**, 16 knots.
Complement, 511.
Guns: Main battery, four 13-in., four 8-in.; fourteen 5-in. rapid-fire; secondary rapid-fire battery, twenty 6-pounders, six 1-pounders, four Colts, two field guns.
Torpedo tubes, four.

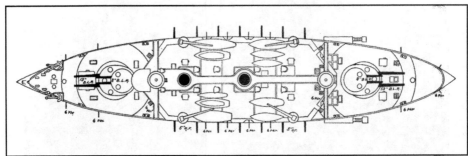

Deck plan of the first-class battleship *Kentucky*

First-class battleships *Kearsarge* and *Kentucky*

USS *Alabama, Illinois* and *Wisconsin*
First-class battleships
Authorized: 1896

Displacement, 11,525 tons.   **Speed**, 16 knots.
Complement, 489.
Guns: Main battery, four 13-in., fourteen 6-in. rapid-fire; secondary rapid-fire battery, sixteen 6-pounders, four 1-pounders, one Colt, two field guns.
Torpedo tubes, four.

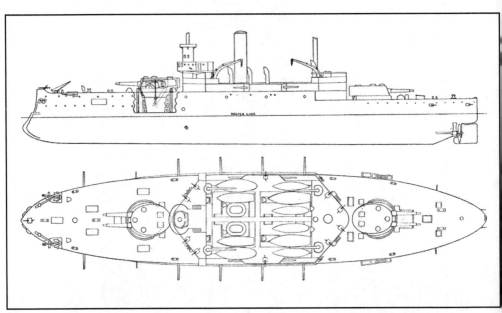

Deck plan and side elevation of the first-class battleship *Alabama*

First-class battleships *Alabama*, *Illinois* and *Wisconsin*

Elliptical turret of the first-class battleship *Alabama*

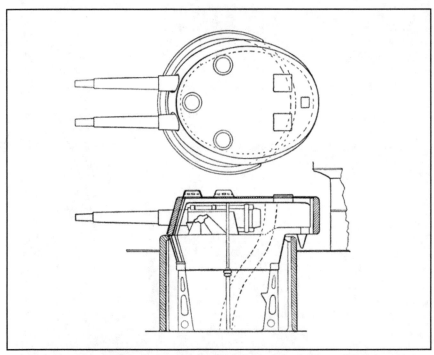

Plan and vertical section through elliptical turret and barbette

2) CRUISERS

USS *Atlanta*
Protected cruiser
Authorized: 1883

Displacement, 3,189 tons.   **Speed**, 16.3 knots.
Complement, 284.
Guns: two 8-in., six 6-in., two 6-pounders, two 3-pounders, two 1-pounders, two Gatlings.

A 6-inch gun

USS *Boston*
Protected cruiser
Authorized: 1883

Displacement, 3,189 tons.   **Speed**, 16.3 knots.
Complement, 284.
Guns: two 8-in., six 6-in., two 6-pounders, two 3-pounders, two 1-pounders, two Gatlings.

At Manila

Departing from New York Harbor
for Europe (1889)

Circa 1890

USS *Chicago*
Protected cruiser
Authorized: 1883

Displacement, 4,500 tons.   **Speed**, 18 knots (estimated).
Complement, 409.
Guns: four 8-in., fourteen rapid-fire 5-in.; secondary rapid-fire battery, seven 6-pounders, two 1-pounders, two Colts, one field gun.

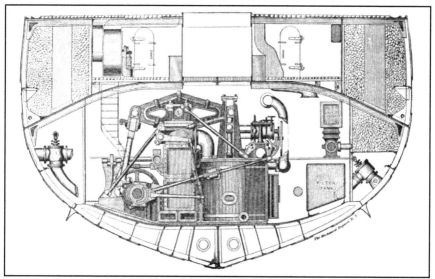

One of *Chicago*'s two original beam-propeller engines

A pair of nickel steel scotch boilers

USS *Charleston*
Protected cruiser
Authorized: 1885

Displacement, 3,730 tons.   **Speed**, 18.2 knots.
Complement, 306.
Guns: Main battery, two 8-in., six 6-in. slow-fire; secondary rapid-fire battery, four 6-pounders, two 3-pounders, two 1-pounders, four 37-mm. Hotchkiss, two Colts, one field gun.

At Manila   At Hong Kong (1898)

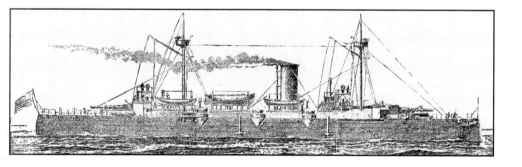

USS *Newark*

Protected cruiser
Authorized: 1885

Displacement, 4,095 tons.   **Speed**, 19 knots.
Complement, 384.
Guns: Main battery, twelve 6-in. rapid-fire; secondary battery, eight 6-pounders, two Colts, two 87-millimeter guns, one 3-inch field gun.

(as reconstructed)

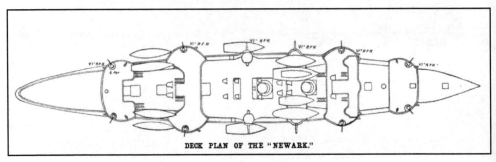

DECK PLAN OF THE "NEWARK."

Marines manning the secondary battery on board the USS *Newark*

Engine room

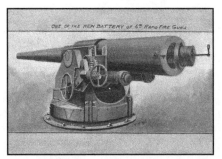

6-inch gun

USS *Baltimore*
Protected cruiser
Authorized: 1886

Displacement, 4,413 tons.   **Speed**, 20.1 knots.
Complement, 386.
Guns: Main battery, four 8-in., six 6-in. slow-fire; secondary rapid-fire battery, four 6-pounders, two 3-pounders, two 1-pounders, four 37-mm. Hotchkiss, two Colts, one field gun.

USS *Baltimore* in action

At Honolulu (1897-1898)

Drying laundry

Le « Baltimore », croiseur américain de 1ʳᵉ classe.

USS *Vesuvius*
Dynamite gun cruiser
Authorized: 1886

Displacement, 929 tons.   **Speed**, 21.42 knots.
Complement, 69.
Guns: three 15-in. dynamite guns, three 3-pounder rapid-fire guns.

A unique vessel in the Navy inventory

1. Positions of boilers, engines, guns, and air reservoirs.   2. Compressed
air reservoirs.   3. Bow view.   4. Boiler room and passageway.
5. Section showing "revolvers," carrying the dynamite shells, and
protective steel deck.   6. Broadside exterior view.
7. Dynamite shell.   Center—The dynamite guns projecting above deck.

Dynamite gun muzzles

The three dynamite guns below deck

USS *San Francisco*

Protected cruiser
Authorized: 1887

Displacement, 4,098 tons.　　**Speed**, 19.5 knots.
Complement, 383.
Guns: Main battery, twelve 6-in. slow-fire; secondary rapid-fire battery, four 6-pounders, four 3-pounders, two 1-pounders, three 37-mm. Hotchkiss, four Gatlings, one field gun.
Torpedo tubes, four.

After the trial trip-record 19.5 knots

Full speed during trial trip—Ship not yet rigged

Protected cruiser *San Francisco* as completed

Passing a stakeboat—The bow wave

Wave-line seen from astern

USS *New York*

Protected cruiser
Authorized: 1888

Displacement, 8,200 tons.   **Speed**, 21 knots.
Complement, 556.
Guns: Main battery, six 8-in., twelve 4-in. rapid-fire; secondary rapid-fire battery, eight 6-pounders, two 1-pounders, four Gatlings, two field guns.
Torpedo tubes, two.

At full speed: 21 knots an hour

Summer 1898

Stern view

USS *Olympia*
Protected cruiser
Authorized: 1888

Displacement, 5,870 tons.   **Speed**, 21.7 knots.
Complement, 450.
Guns: Main battery, four 8-in., ten rapid-fire 5-in.; secondary rapid-fire
battery, fourteen 6-pounders, seven 1-pounders, four Gatlings, one field
gun.
Torpedo tubes, five.

Making 22.26 knots

Plaque on *Olympia*

U.S.S. Olympia. Boston Feb.10, 1902. 3-27-12

USS *Cincinnati*
Protected cruiser
Authorized: 1888

Displacement, 3,213 tons.   **Speed**, 19 knots.
Complement, 314.
Guns: Main battery, one slow-fire 6-in., ten rapid-fire 5-in.; secondary rapid-fire battery, eight 6-pounders, two 1-pounders, two Colts, one field gun.
Torpedo tubes, two.

USS *Detroit*

Unprotected cruiser
Authorized: 1888

Displacement, 2,089 tons.   **Speed**, 18.7 knots.
Complement, 256.
Guns: Main battery, ten rapid-fire 5-in.; secondary rapid-fire battery, six 6-pounders, two 1-pounders, two Colts, one field gun.
Torpedo tubes, two.

USS *Columbia*
Protected cruiser
Authorized: 1890

Displacement, 7,375 tons.   **Speed**, 22.8 knots.
Complement, 556.
Guns: Main battery, one 8-in.; two 6-in. slow-fire, eight rapid-fire 4-in.; secondary rapid-fire battery, twelve 6-pounders, four 1-pounders, two Colts, one field gun.
Torpedo tubes, four.

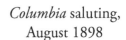

Columbia saluting,
August 1898

In dry dock n° 2 Brooklyn Navy Yard

Columbia in 1898

In dry dock n° 2 Brooklyn Navy Yard,
showing the arrangement of triple screws

Night patrol

USS *Philadelphia*
Protected cruiser
Commissioned: 1890

Displacement, 4,324 tons.   **Speed**, 19 knots.
Complement, 384.
Guns: Twelve 6-in./30 caliber breech-loading rifles; four 6-pounders; four 3-pounders; two 1-pounders, two Gatling gun.

About 1892

USS *Minneapolis*
Protected cruiser
Authorized: 1891

Displacement, 7,375 tons.   **Speed**, 23.07 knots.
Complement, 556.
Guns: Main battery, one 8-in., two 6-in. slow-fire, eight rapid-fire 4-in.;
secondary battery, twelve 6-pounders, four 1-pounders, two Colts, one
field gun.
Torpedo tubes, four.

On trials, 1894

Summer 1898

USS *Brooklyn*
Protected cruiser
Authorized: 1892

Displacement, 9,215 tons.   **Speed**, 21.9 knots.
Complement, 516.
Guns: Main battery, eight 8-in., twelve 5-in. rapid-fire; secondary battery, twelve 6-pounders, four 1-pounders, four Colts, two field guns.
Torpedo tubes, four.

In New York Harbor, summer 1898

Returning to the US

At fleet review

Bow view

Crew and goat

At Santiago

Forward 8-inch gun and
the military mast of the *Brooklyn*,
where commodore Schley will be
stationed during a fight

USS *Raleigh*
Protected cruiser
Commissioned: 1894

Displacement, 3,183 tons.   **Speed**, 19 knots.
Complement, 302.
Guns: One 6-in./40 caliber; ten 5-in./40 caliber; eight 6-pounders, two 1-pounders.
Torpedo tubes, four.

USS *Marblehead*
Unprotected cruiser
Commissioned: 1894

Displacement, 2,072 tons.   **Speed**, 18 knots.
Complement, 279.
Guns: Two 6-in./40 caliber; eight 5-in./40 caliber; six 6-pounders, two 1-pounders; two Gatling guns.
Torpedo tubes, three.

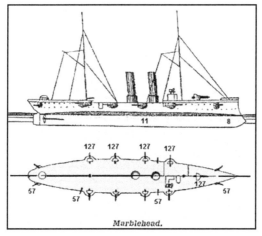

Marblehead.

USS *Albany*

Protected cruiser
Acquired: 16 March 1898,
to prevent her from being acquired
by the Spanish Navy during
the Spanish-American War.
She saw service in
the Philippine-American War.

Displacement, 3,428 tons.   **Speed**, 20.52 knots.
Complement, 363.
Guns: Six 6-in.; four 4.7-in.; ten 6-pounder Hotchkiss guns; four 1-pounders.
Torpedo tubes, three.

In dry drock,
Boston, Massachusetts

At Santa Monica,
California, 1909

USS *New Orleans*
Protected cruiser
Authorized: 1898

Displacement, 3,600 tons.   **Speed**, 21.05 knots.
Complement, 350.
Guns: Main battery, six 6-in. rapid-fire, four 4.7-in. rapid-fire; secondary rapid-fire battery, ten 6-pounders, four 1-pounders, four machine guns.
Torpedo tubes, three.

When first purchased

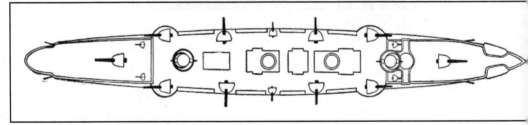

Deck plan

Cruisers

During the war

Dressed with flags

In 1899

6 inch gun on cruiser USS *New Orleans*. This is a non-standard gun in US Navy service : an Elswick Ordnance (British) 50-caliber QF gun (note coned breech screw) acquired with USS *New Orleans* (ex-*Amazonas*) and USS *Albany* (ex-*Almirante Abreu*).

Hart, Edward H., photographer. Detroit Publishing Co., publisher. Gift to LOC; State Historical Society of Colorado; 1949.

Source: Wikimedia Commons

At Brooklyn Navy yard, 1898

Comparison between protected cruisers, armored cruisers and battleships

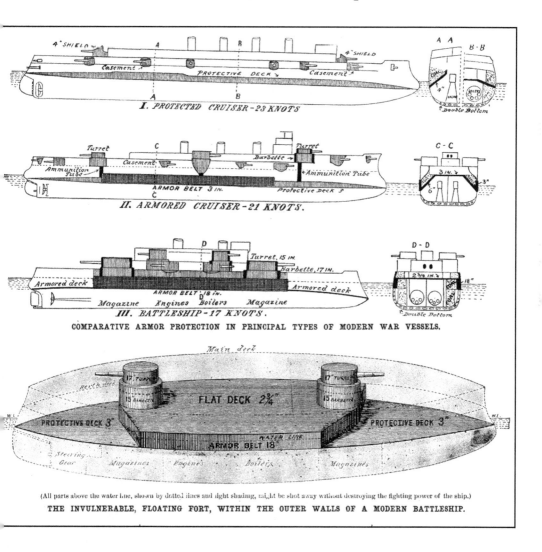

COMPARATIVE ARMOR PROTECTION IN PRINCIPAL TYPES OF MODERN WAR VESSELS.

(All parts above the water line, shown by dotted lines and light shading, might be shot away without destroying the fighting power of the ship.)

THE INVULNERABLE, FLOATING FORT, WITHIN THE OUTER WALLS OF A MODERN BATTLESHIP.

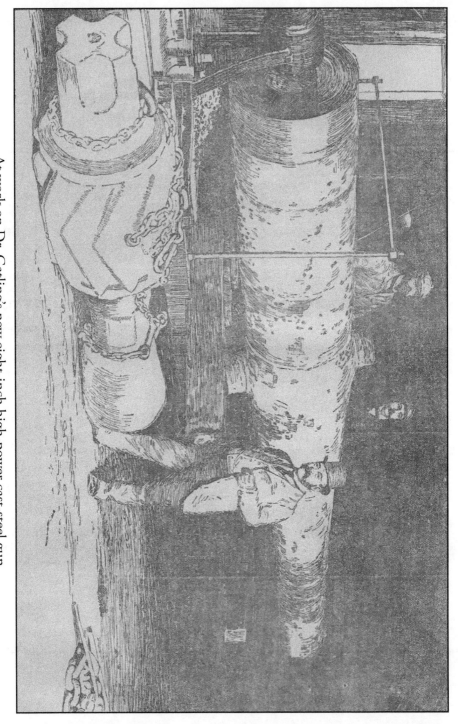

At work on Dr. Gatling's new eight-inch high-power cast-steel gun

3) OTHER SHIPS

USS *Amphitrite*
Monitor
Authorized: 1885

Displacement, 3,990 tons.   **Speed**, 10.5 knots.
Complement, 182.
Guns: Main battery, four 10-in., two rapid-fire 4-in. rapid-fire; secondary rapid-fire battery, two 6-pounders, two 3-pounders, two 37-mm. Hotchkiss, two 1-pounders.

At Boston Navy Yard

The forward pair of 10-inch guns

Pneumatic lift for loading charge
into cage of ammunition host

Pneumatic steering apparatus

USS *Monterey*
Monitor
Authorized: 1887

Displacement, 4,084 tons.   **Speed**, 13.6 knots.
Complement, 195.
Guns: Main battery, two 12-in., two 10-in.; secondary rapid-fire battery, six 6-pounders, four 1-pounders, two Gatlings.

Off Mare Island

En route for Manila

Triple expansion engines of the new United States
armored coast defense vessel *Monterey*

USS *Petrel*
Gunboat
Launched: 1888

Displacement, 867 tons.   **Speed**, 11.4 knots.
Complement, 195.
Guns: four 6-in., two 3-pounders, one 1-pounder.

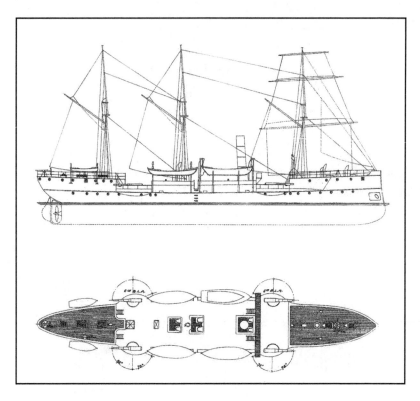

PETREL.
Cañonero protegido

As seen by the Spaniards in
Blunco y Negro (May 1898)

USS *Katahdin*
Armored ram
Authorized: 1889

Displacement, 2,155 tons.   **Speed**, 16.11 knots.
Complement, 97.
Guns: four 6-pounder rapid-firers.

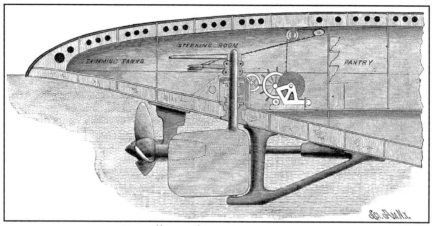

Propeller and steering apparatus

Cross section
amidships

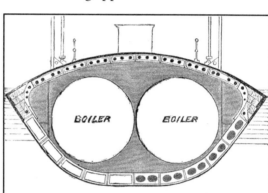

Longitudinal
section of stem

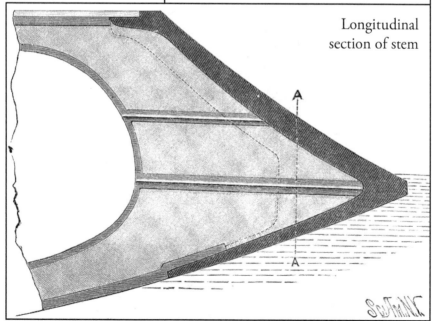

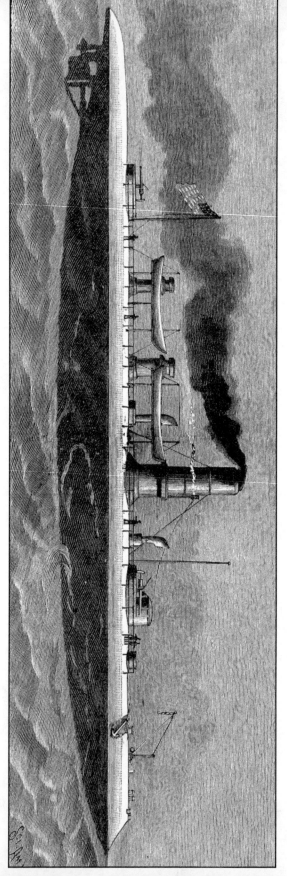

At the time of the war, the *USS Katahdin* was the only vessel of its type in the world. Held in reserve for possible harbor defense, it never had an opportunity to display its efficiency.

USS *Miantonomoh*
Monitor
Authorized: 1891

Displacement, 3,990 tons.   **Speed**, 10.6 knots.
Complement, 150.
Guns: four 10-in., two 4-in., two 6-pounders.

1. Side view.   2. Under headway.   3. Interior of conning tower.
4. Cross section of turret and hull.

TORPEDO-BOAT BEING DISCOVERED BY USE OF SEARCH-LIGHT ON U. S. S. MIANTONOMAH.

USS *Helena*
Gunboat
Authorized: 1893

Displacement, 1,392 tons.   **Speed**, 15.50 knots.
Complement, 175.
Guns: Main battery, eight 4-in. rapid-fire; secondary rapid-fire battery, four 6-pounders, four 1-pounders, two Colts, one field gun.

Dressed
with flags

USS *Merrimac*
Collier

Displacement, 3,362 tons.

The USS *Merrimac* was the only American vessel sunk by the Spanish navy during the conflict.

Le « Merrimac ».

The wreck, 2 June 1898

USS *Annapolis*
Composite gunboat
Authorized: 1895

Displacement, 1,000 tons.   **Speed**, 13.17 knots.
Complement, 135.
Guns: Main battery, six 4-in. rapid-fire guns; secondary battery, four 6-pounders, two 1-pounders, one Colt, one field gun.

USS *Marietta*
Composite gunboat
Authorized: 1895

Displacement, 1,000 tons.   **Speed**, 13.03 knots.
Complement, 140.
Guns: Main battery, six 4-in. rapid-fire guns; secondary battery, four 6-pounders, two 1-pounders, one Colt, one field gun.

USS *Puritan*
Monitor
Commissioned: 1896

Displacement, 6,060 tons.   **Speed**, 12.4 knots.
Complement, 200.
Guns: Four 12-in. breechloader rifles; six 4-in. breechloader rifles;
6-pounder guns.

At Matanzas

USS *Porter*

First-class torpedo boat
Authorized: 1895

Displacement, 190 tons.   **Speed**, 28.63 knots.
Complement, 32.
Armament: Three 18-in. Whitehead torpedo tubes; four 1-pounder rapid-fire guns.

On her trial trip

USS *Bailey*
Torpedo boat destroyer
Authorized: 1897

Displacement, 235 tons.   **Speed**, 30 knots.
Complement, 40.
Armament: Two 18-in. Whitehead discharge tubes, four 6-pounder rapid-fire guns.

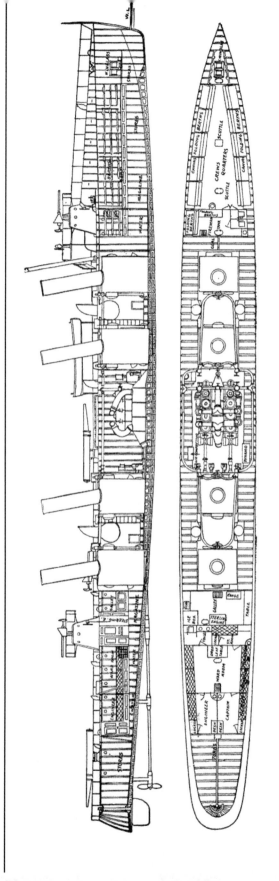

USS *Bailey*

Longitudinal section and plan of the *Bailey*

USS *Concord*
Gunboat
Recommissioned: 1897

Displacement, 1,710 tons.   **Speed**, 16.8 knots.
Complement, 193.
Armament: Six 6-in./30 caliber Mark 3 guns; two 6-pounder guns; two 3-pounder guns; two 1-pounder guns.

At Manila Bay

USS *Wilmington*
Gunboat
Commissioned: 1897

Displacement, 1,571 tons.   **Speed**, 13 knots.
Complement, 212.
Armament: Eight 4-in. guns, four 3-pounder guns.

On the Orinoco

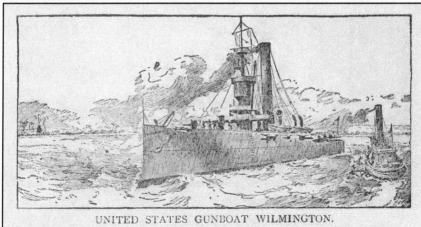

UNITED STATES GUNBOAT WILMINGTON.

USS *Lehigh*
Monitor
Commissioned: 1863

Displacement, 1,335 tons.　　**Speed**, 11.6 knots.
Complement, 88.
Armament: One 15-in. smoothbore; one 8-in. Parrott rifle.

During the
Spanish-American War

On the James River,
Virginia, between
ca. 1860 and 1865

USS *Monadnock*
Monitor of the *Amphitrite* class
Launched: 1883
Commissioned: 1896

Displacement, 3,990 tons.   **Speed**, 11.6 knots.
Complement, 156.
Armament: Four 10-in. caliber guns; two 4-in. guns; two 6-pounder guns; two 3-pounder guns; two 1-pounder gun.

The coast defense monitor *Monadnock* starting for Manila

Crossing the Pacific Ocean during the Spanish-American War

In Chinese waters, ca. 1901

USS *Nahant*
Monitor
Commissioned: 1862

Displacement, 1,875 tons.   **Speed**, 5 knots.
Complement, 75.
Armament: One 15-in. smoothbore; one 11-in. Dahlgren gun.

At New York, 1898

USS *Nahant* wabbing out gun and mending the flag

USS *Ajax*
Monitor
Commissioned: 1871

Displacement, 1,034 tons.   **Speed**, 8 knots.
Complement, 100.
Armament: Two 15-in. smoothbore Dahlgren guns.

USS *McCulloch*

Cruising cutter
Commissioned: 1897

Displacement, 1,432 tons.   **Speed**, 17 knots.
Complement, 130.
Armament: Four 3-in. guns; one torpedo tube.

USS *Princeton*
Gunboat
Commissioned: 1898

Displacement, 1,103 tons.   **Speed**, 11 knots.
Complement, 147.
Armament: Two 1-pounder guns; one machine gun.

In the Philippines, about 1903

USS *Machias*
Gunboat
Commissioned: 1893

Displacement, 1,177 tons.   **Speed**, 15.5 knots.
Complement, 154.
Armament: Eight 4-in. guns; four 6-pounder guns; four 1-pounder gun.

USS *Castine*
Gunboat
Commissioned: 1894

Displacement, 1,177 tons.   **Speed**, 15.5 knots.
Complement, 154.
Armament: Eight 4-in. guns; four 6-pounder guns.

U. S. S. CASTINE.

USS *Topeka*
Gunboat
Commissioned: 1898

Displacement, 2,255 tons.   **Speed**, 16 knots.
Complement, 167.
Armament: Six 4-in. guns; six 3-pounder guns; two 1-pounder guns; one Colt machine gun.

Off the New York Navy Yard, 1898

USS *Winslow*
Torpedo boat
Commissioned: 1897

Displacement, 142 tons.   **Speed**, 25 knots.
Complement, 20.
Armament: Three 1-pounder guns; three torpedo tubes.

Off Philadelphia, 1898

Battle damage to *Winslow*'s
conning tower

USS *Cushing*
Torpedo boat
Commissioned: 1890

Displacement, 105 tons.   **Speed**, 23 knots.
Complement, 22.
Armament: Two 6-pounder guns; three torpedo tubes.

Marina de guerra norteamericana.—EL TORPEDERO «CUSHING», DE 105 TONELADAS

USS *Talbot*
Torpedo boat
Commissioned: 1898

Displacement, 46 tons.   **Speed**, 21.5 knots.
Complement, 16.
Armament: One 1-pounder gun; one torpedo tube.

USS *Cushing*
torpedo boat
experiments,
ca. 1890

USS *Bancroft*
Gunboat
Commissioned: 1893

Displacement, 839 tons.　　**Speed**, 14.3 knots.
Complement, 130.
Armament: Four 4-in. guns; two 6-pounder guns; two 3-pounder guns; one 1-pounder gun; one 37-mm Hotchkiss revolving cannon; one Gatling gun.

Firing a salute, 1898

USS *Dolphin*
Gunboat/dispatch vessel
Commissioned: 1885

Displacement, 1,485 tons.   **Speed**, 16 knots.
Complement, 152.
Armament: One 6-in./30 caliber Mark gun; two 6-pounder guns;
four 3-pounder Hotchkiss revolving cannon.

USS *Nashville*
Gunboat
Commissioned: 1897

Displacement, 1,371 tons.   **Speed**, 16.3 knots.
Complement, 180.
Armament: Eight 4-in. guns; two 6-pounder guns; two 3-pounder guns; two 1-pounder guns.

Circa the early 1900s

USS *Windom*
(later named *Comanche*)
Revenue cutter
Commissioned: 1896

Displacement, 535 tons.   **Speed**, 15 knots.
Complement, 49.
Armament: One 3-in. gun; two 6-pounder guns.

USS *Holland*

Submarine torpedo boat
Launched: 1897
Acquired and commissioned: 1900
(She did not participate in the war but was
the first modern commissioned submarine)

Speed, 30 knots.   **Complement**, 6.
Armament: One Whitehead discharge tube, one aerial dynamite-gun,
one under-water dynamite gun.

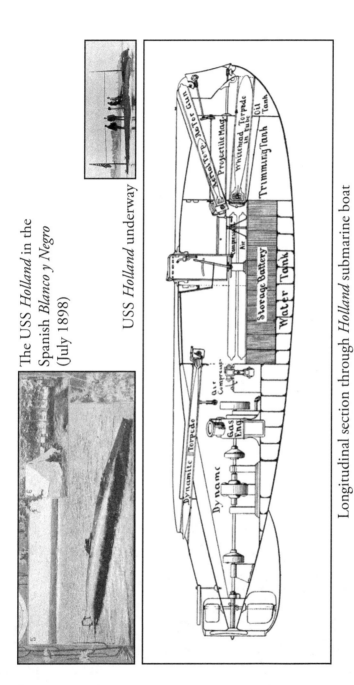

The USS *Holland* in the Spanish *Blanco y Negro* (July 1898)

USS *Holland* underway

Longitudinal section through *Holland* submarine boat

141

Rough sketch

Conning tower

Dynamite gun tubes

Aerial torpedo

Whitehead torpedo

Aft ballast

Gasoline engine

Main ballast

Storage battery

Oil tank

USS *Maine*
Authorized: 1886

We started our gallery with the *Maine*, and we finish it with her **torpedo boat**.

Displacement, 15 tons.   **Speed**, 18 knots.
Complement, 5 men.
Armament: One 18-in. Whitehead torpedo tube, one 1-pounder rapid-fire gun.

Torpedo boats for the cruiser *Maine*

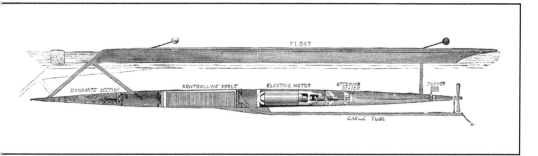

The Sims-Edison Torpedo

Discharging a Whitehead Torpedo

"OUR NAVY AS IT IS TO-DAY"

1. Monadnock 2. Petrel 3. Puritan 4. Concord 5. Wilmington 6. Amphitrite 7. Ajax
8. Machias 9. Cincinnati 10. Marblehead 11. Montgomery 12. Minneapolis 13. Kearsarge
14. Kentucky 15. Bancroft 16. Dolphin 17. Vesuvius 18. Raleigh 19. Indiana 20. Iowa
21. Olympia 22. Terror 23. Catskill 24. Miantonomoh 25. Castine 26. Yorktown
27. Texas 28. Helena 29. Massachusetts 30. Columbia 31. New Orleans 32. San Francisco
33. Canonicus 34. Comanche 35. Monterey 36. Brooklyn 37. Detroit 38. Atlanta
39. Alabama 40. Albany 41. Baltimore 42. Chicago 43. Newark 44. Boston 45. Charleston
46. Oregon 47. New York 48. Manhattan 49. Philadelphia 50. Lehigh.
And Torpedo Boats.—Drawn by W.A. Verhas for *The New York Ledger*.

146

FINAL IMAGES

USS *Montgomery,*
unprotected cruiser

USS *Canonicus,*
single-turret monitor

USS *Catskill,*
single-turret monitor

The dispatch boat *Fern*

USS *Bennington,*
gunboat

USS *Bennington,*
in drydock

USS *Gloucester*,
gunboat

Seneca,
transport of troops

The improved Gatling gun-navy model (1895)

UNITED STATES BATTLESHIP INDIANA

UNITED STATES BATTLESHIP IOWA

UNITED STATES ARMORED CRUISER NEW YORK

UNITED STATES BATTLESHIP TEXAS

UNITED STATES ARMORED CRUISER BROOKLYN

UNITED STATES PROTECTED CRUISER COLUMBIA

UNITED STATES MONITOR MIANTONOMOH

UNITED STATES TORPEDO BOAT CUSHING

Les principaux bâtiments de la flotte des Etats-Unis. — (Voir l'article, page 300.)

UNCLE SAM'S NEW DESTROYERS
Bought by This Government in France, It Is Hurrying Across the Atlantic to Strengthen Our Torpedo Fleet

THREE VESSELS WHICH WILL SOON BE PART OF OUR NAVY

THE ST LOUIS

Com S B Sborn

THE NITCHEROY

Capt C F Goodrich

THE ST PAUL

BY THE USE OF THE TELEPHONE KITE OUR WARSHIPS CAN TALK AT SEA.

BIRD'S EYE VIEW OF THE SHIPBUILDING YARD OF WILLIAM CRAMP & SONS, SHOWING WAR VESSELS CONSTRUCTED BY THEM.

The USS *Olympia* today, as a museum ship

TO KNOW MORE ABOUT THESE SHIPS

- Library of Congress
- Naval History and Heritage Command (www.history.navy.mil)
- NavSource Naval History (www.navsource.org)
- Navypedia (www.navypedia.org)
  Reference data about all fighting ships of all Navies served since 1900.
- The Spanish American War Centennial Website! (www.spanamwar.com)
- Wreck Site (www.wrecksite.eu)
- Wikipedia
- An interesting list of books about the Spanish-American War can be found on the website of the Library of Congress in "World of 1898."

COLUMBIA'S NEW EASTER BONNET.
From the *Tribune* (Minneapolis).

ALPHABETICAL INDEX OF SHIPS

CPSIA information can be obtained
at www.ICGtesting.com
Printed in the USA
BVHW03s1927260218
509141BV00002B/25/P